PICTU

 **Specific Skill Series**
for Reading

Finding Details

Sixth Edition

Columbus, OH

The McGraw·Hill Companies

Cover: © Randy Faris/Corbis

SRAonline.com

 SRA

Send all inquiries to:
SRA/McGraw-Hill
8787 Orion Place
Columbus, OH 43240-4027

ISBN 0-07-603991-9

1 2 3 4 5 6 7 8 9 BCH 12 11 10 09 08 07 06 05

TO THE TEACHER

PURPOSE:

FINDING DETAILS is designed to develop skill in recalling details from a single reading. The material is structured so students cannot "look back" for the answer. The story is on one side; the questions are on the reverse. Readers must take as much as they can from one reading. The knowledge that they cannot turn back to the story helps them gain skill in **FINDING DETAILS.**

FOR WHOM:

The skill of **FINDING DETAILS** is developed through a series of books spanning ten levels (Picture, Preparatory, A, B, C, D, E, F, G, H). The Picture Level is for students who have not acquired a basic sight vocabulary. The Preparatory Level is for students who have a basic sight vocabulary but are not quite ready for the first-grade-level book. Books A through H are appropriate for students who can read on levels one through eight, respectively.

THE NEW EDITION:

The sixth edition of the *Specific Skill Series for Reading* maintains the quality and focus that has distinguished this program for more than 40 years. A key element central to the program's success has been the unique nature of the reading selections. Fiction and nonfiction pieces about current topics have been designed to stimulate the interest of students, motivating them to use the comprehension strategies they have learned to further their reading. To keep this important aspect of the program intact, a percentage of the reading selections has been replaced in order to ensure the continued relevance of the subject material.

In addition, a significant percentage of the artwork in the program has been replaced to give the books a contemporary look. The cover photographs are designed to appeal to readers of all ages.

SESSIONS:

Short practice sessions are the most effective. It is desirable to have a practice session every day or every other day, using a few units each session.

SCORING:

Students should record their answers on the reproducible worksheets. The worksheets make scoring easier and provide uniform records of the students' work. Using worksheets also avoids consuming the exercise books.

It is important for students to know how well they are doing. For this reason, units should be scored as soon as they have been completed. Then a discussion can be held in which students justify their choices. (The *Language Activity Pages,* many of which are open-ended, do not lend themselves to an objective score; thus there are no answer keys for these pages.)

GENERAL INFORMATION ON *FINDING DETAILS:*

FINDING DETAILS varies in content. It contains both fiction and nonfiction stories that will help stretch the imagination, spark new hobbies, promote admiration for outstanding achievements, and develop a sense of wonder about our world.

There is only one correct answer for each question. Students practice recalling details they read or saw in a picture. **FINDING DETAILS** helps students' comprehension as they carefully read the question and choose the answer that correctly states a detail found in the selection.

SUGGESTED STEPS:

1. Students read the story. (In the Picture Level books, the students look at the pictures.)
2. After completing the story, students turn to the questions on the reverse side and choose the letters of the correct answers.
3. Students write the letters of the correct answers on the worksheets.
4. Students may return to the story only after their answers have been recorded and scored.

RELATED MATERIALS:

Specific Skill Series Assessment Book provides the teacher with a pretest and posttest for each skill at each grade level. These tests will help the teacher assess students' growth performance in each of the nine comprehension skills.

About This Book

A **detail** is additional information about something or someone. Each of the following sentences gives a detail:

A dog has four legs.

Apples grow on trees.

You can look for details when you read. You can look for details in a picture too. Look at this picture:

These are details about the picture:

There are three girls.

They are playing with a ball.

There are twenty-five units in this book. For each unit, you will see three pictures on one page. Look at the pictures carefully. Think about what each picture shows. Then turn the page. Answer the questions about the pictures.

1.

2.

3.

1. The boy had a
   (A) party.
   (B) bike.

---

2. The boy cut the
   (A) tree.
   (B) cake.

---

3. The boys and girls
   (A) ate.
   (B) hid.

1.

2.

3.

1. The man went in a
   (A) car.
   (B) boat.

---

2. The man was
   (A) reading.
   (B) fishing.

---

3. The man got a
   (A) hat.
   (B) coat.

1.

2.

3.

1. The girls were

    (A) working.

    (B) playing.

---

2. The girls

    (A) ran.

    (B) walked.

---

3. The girls

    (A) had fun.

    (B) got wet.

1.

2.

3.

1. The boy was

   (A) watching television.

   (B) reading a book.

---

2. The dog

   (A) jumped on the boy.

   (B) ran away.

---

3. The boy

   (A) petted the dog.

   (B) put the dog out.

1.

2.

3.

1. The girl was
   (A) painting.
   (B) riding.

---

2. The boy
   (A) played with the girl.
   (B) talked to the girl.

---

3. The boy
   (A) helped the girl.
   (B) went down the street.

1.

2.

3.

1. The boy liked his toy
   (A) train.
   (B) airplane.

2. The boy
   (A) worked.
   (B) played.

3. The toy went into a
   (A) car.
   (B) house.

A. Exercising Your Skill

Look at the picture. Tell a classmate all the facts about it.

Knowing what time it is helps you know when to have lunch. When else do you need to know what time it is?

B. Expanding Your Skill

Pretend you are the school clock or your watch. Tell all the facts you can think of about yourself.

Did you tell your size? Color? Shape? The sound you make? What your numbers are like? How you move? What time you are showing? Where you are?

C. Exploring Language

Listen to the facts. Tell the correct time of day for each one.

noon   seven o'clock   nine o'clock

1. Emily is brushing her teeth. It is dark out. Soon she will go to bed. It is ___ at night.

2. Emily is eating eggs and toast. The school bus will be here soon. It is ___ in the morning.

3. Emily is hungry. Soon she will take her lunch to the cafeteria. It is ___.

D. Expressing Yourself

Do one of these things.

1. Draw a clock. Then draw a picture to show what you do at the time shown on the clock.

2. Tell the class about your favorite time of day.

1.

2.

3.

1. Miss Han went
   (A) to bed.
   (B) into a house.

2. Miss Han saw a
   (A) fire.
   (B) cat.

3. Miss Han
   (A) ran out of the house.
   (B) put out the fire.

1.

2.

3.

1. The girl saw a toy
 (A) car.
 (B) airplane.

2. The girl
 (A) got into the car.
 (B) painted the car.

3. The girl
 (A) played with the car.
 (B) lost the car.

1.

2.

3.

1. The boy was
   (A) fishing.
   (B) eating.

2. The boy
   (A) walked.
   (B) ran.

3. The boy went
   (A) up a tree.
   (B) into a school.

1.

2.

3.

1. The boy saw a pig
   (A) jump from a truck.
   (B) on television.

---

2. The pig
   (A) ran away.
   (B) ran to the boy.

---

3. The pig
   (A) sat in the road.
   (B) went around the house.

1.

2.

3.

1. The boy was looking for a
   (A) book.
   (B) toy.

---

2. The boy went to
   (A) see his mother.
   (B) bed.

---

3. The boy
   (A) read.
   (B) played.

1.

2.

3.

1. The girl made a
   (A) boat.
   (B) bowl of spaghetti.

---

2. The dog began to
   (A) watch television.
   (B) eat the spaghetti.

---

3. The girl was
   (A) not happy.
   (B) happy.

A. Exercising Your Skill

What can a weather report tell you? Answer *Yes* or *No* to tell if a weather reporter knows about each one.

1. If it will rain tomorrow
2. What time the sun sets today
3. How many stop signs are in your town
4. What the temperature is outdoors

B. Expanding Your Skill

Listen to each sentence. Choose the job that answers each question.

vet   farmer   nurse   teacher

1. Who grows our food?

2. Who takes care of sick children?

3. Who teaches children to read?

4. Who helps sick animals?

C. Exploring Language

Listen to the details.

Kate is a woodworker. She cuts wood with a saw. She puts boards together with a hammer and nails. Today she made a table.

Look at the list of tools below. Tell the name of Kate's job. Add one more tool to the list.

nails

saw

_____

D. Expressing Yourself

Do one of these things.

1. Find a picture of a job in a magazine. Tell the facts about the picture.

2. Act out what someone does on the job. Have your classmates guess what job you are acting out.

1.

2.

3.

1. The boy played with the
   (A) truck.
   (B) baby.

2. The boy made the baby
   (A) laugh.
   (B) fall.

3. The boy made the baby
   (A) sing.
   (B) cry.

1.

2.

3.

1. The dog was on
   (A) the sidewalk.
   (B) a boat.

---

2. The boy took the dog
   (A) to a zoo.
   (B) into the house.

---

3. The boy
   (A) did not help the dog.
   (B) helped the dog.

1.

2.

3.

1. The girl went for a
   (A) ride.
   (B) walk.

---

2. The girl went to a
   (A) market.
   (B) movie theater.

---

3. The girl got something to
   (A) eat.
   (B) read.

1.

2.

3.

1. The boy went
  (A) up a tree.
  (B) to a show.

---

2. The boy
  (A) painted a boat.
  (B) called for help.

---

3. The dad helped his son
  (A) go up.
  (B) get down.

1.

2.

3.

1. The boy was
   (A) playing ball.
   (B) walking down a street.

---

2. The boy went
   (A) behind the fence.
   (B) to bed.

---

3. The boy
   (A) jumped on the dog.
   (B) petted the dog.

1.

2.

3.

1. The girl went
  (A) to a farm.
  (B) into a house.

---

2. The girl saw
  (A) cats running.
  (B) goats eating.

---

3. The girl ran away from a
  (A) dog.
  (B) pig.

1.

2.

3.

1. The man was
   (A) working.
   (B) fishing.

---

2. It started to
   (A) rain.
   (B) snow.

---

3. The man ran to a
   (A) boat.
   (B) house.

A. Exercising Your Skill

Look at the picture.

Play Mother, May I? Raise your hand, and wait to be called on. Take one giant step for every detail you can tell about the picture.

B. Expanding Your Skill

Pick a partner. Study each other for a few moments. Turn back to back. Say as many details as you can remember about your partner. You can score one point for each correct detail.

C. Exploring Language

Read the details. Say the name of someone in your class who fits each set of details.

1. I have black hair and brown eyes.	2. My pants are blue.
3. I am sitting near the teacher.	4. I am wearing white socks.

D. Expressing Yourself

Stand in front of the class. Then go out of the room. Change one thing about yourself, and come back. See who can name the change.

1.

2.

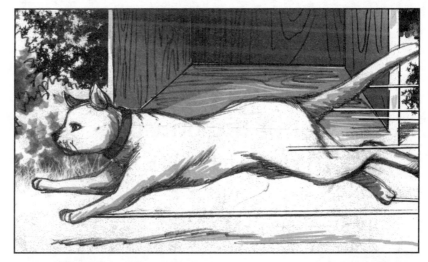

3.

1. The cat got a new
   (A) coat.
   (B) collar.

2. The cat ran
   (A) out of the house.
   (B) to the girl.

3. The cat sat
   (A) on a car.
   (B) in a tree.

1.

2.

3.

1. The boy was
   (A) riding a bike.
   (B) walking.

---

2. The boy stopped to
   (A) eat.
   (B) talk.

---

3. The boy
   (A) helped his friend.
   (B) went swimming.

1.

2.

3.

1. The woman was painting a
   (A) playhouse.
   (B) wagon.

---

2. The dog put its paws on the
   (A) tree.
   (B) playhouse.

---

3. The dog ran
   (A) into the house.
   (B) down the road.

1.

2.

3.

1. The boys and girls were
  (A) eating.
  (B) working.

---

2. The boys and girls began to
  (A) sing.
  (B) run.

---

3. The boys and girls got
  (A) into a car.
  (B) wet.

1.

2.

3.

1. The girl came out of a
   (A) school.
   (B) house.

2. The girl
   (A) had a bike.
   (B) walked home.

3. The girl went into
   (A) her house.
   (B) a store.

1.

2.

3.

1. The woman went to a
  (A) zoo.
  (B) store.

---

2. The woman got some
  (A) books.
  (B) food.

---

3. The woman went
  (A) swimming.
  (B) home.

A. Exercising Your Skill

Look at the picture. After each sentence say *T* if a sentence is true. Say *N* if it is not true.

1. The animal can fly.
2. The animal can jump.
3. The animal is very skinny.
4. The animal has a curly tail.
5. The animal is a pig.

B. Expanding Your Skill

Make up animal riddles. Tell three facts about an animal. See who can guess what it is.

C. Exploring Language

Draw a picture of an animal. Pick four of the parts below to include in your picture.

paw	hoof	ear
whiskers	tail	wing
nose	eye	teeth
claw	beak	fur

D. Expressing Yourself

Do one of these things.

1. Pick your favorite pet. Tell three facts about the pet.

2. Tell three facts about how to care for a pet. Make a poster to show how.